T0380699

There are Angels on my Stoep

Dalene Bruwer, Madelie Jansen & Mario Jansen

Balboa Press books may be ordered through booksellers or by contacting:

Balboa Press
A Division of Hay House
1663 Liberty Drive
Bloomington, IN 47403
www.balboapress.com
1 (877) 407-4847

Because of the dynamic nature of the Internet, any web addresses or links contained in this book may have changed since publication and may no longer be valid. The views expressed in this work are solely those of the author and do not necessarily reflect the views of the publisher, and the publisher hereby disclaims any responsibility for them.

Any people depicted in stock imagery provided by Getty Images are models, and such images are being used for illustrative purposes only.
Certain stock imagery © Getty Images.

ISBN: 978-1-9822-3439-3 (sc)
ISBN: 978-1-9822-3440-9 (e)

Print information available on the last page.

Balboa Press rev. date: 09/04/2019

BALBOA.
PRESS
A DIVISION OF HAY HOUSE

CONTENTS

Somehow, somewhere

An angel was calling with something to share

An angel was talking to me

But how could this be

An angel talking to me?

Am i mad

Am i crazy

Am i sad?

Or maybe i am just blessed

To hear an angel talking to me!

-Maddy Jansen

CHAPTER ONE
The angels on *my* *stoep

Meaning of "stoep" – Patio or Veranda

I am a single parent of two gifted children, Mario and Maddy, who are blessed with some of the special gifts written about in the Bible in Corinthians 12 verses 1 to 10:*"The Spirit gives one person the ability to speak with wisdom. The same Spirit gives another person the ability to speak with knowledge. ⁹ To another person the same Spirit gives courageous* faith. *To another person the same Spirit gives the ability to heal. ¹⁰ Another can work miracles. Another can speak what God has revealed. Another can tell the difference between spirits. Another can speak in different kinds of languages. Another can interpret languages."*

And in 1 Corinthians 13 verse 1:*"I may speak in the languages of humans and of angels......."*

One day, while I was sitting on my stoep, after deciding to write this book, I closed my eyes to ponder where to start. I opened my eyes and looked at my two children, laughing and talking and having fun. This is where our story begins, with my two children, my 'angels' on earth, Mario and Maddy, who can feel and see and communicate with the spiritual world.

Mario is the calm and patient one. He is now 32 years old and very wise. When he speaks one cannot help but listen to what he says. He can talk to me or his friends for hours, sharing his wisdom. Although he is assertive he also knows how to listen. When you ask him a question, any question, he will concentrate and contemplate how to answer, even if it is about something mundane, like how his day went. The meaningfulness of his words is very important to him.

Maddy is 25 years old and full of ups and downs. Sometimes she is too quiet and other times she talks and laughs non–stop. It seems as if she is not really comfortable in her own skin because she does not know how to handle her gifts.

It is very difficult for her to trust someone sufficiently in order to share her gifts. She is afraid of being judged or rejected. This is actually not surprising to me, because I feel the same way about their gifts, and that is why I decided to write this book, with their assistance.

Mario and Maddy are like the flip sides of a coin, with two total different personalities. However, they are alike when it comes to their spiritual gifts, they can feel and see and talk and walk with angels, like two peas in a pod.

Mario was diagnosed with dyslexia when he started school. Consequently, from the very beginning of his school years he had problems with spelling and his handwriting was, and still is, almost illegible. Since he is intellectually gifted, he overcame the spelling problem by learning how to spell each and every word. I remember a teacher once wrote in his book that he 'writes like a pig'. In school he was a loner with very few friends. Some thought of him as a weird kid. He was about 18 years old when he told me that he could see spirits. You can imagine what a shock it was to me. I immediately phoned a friend who was a psychologist, to tell him about this revelation.

The first thing my friend asked, was, 'Are they friendly spirits?'

'I think so,' I answered.

He then told me to sit tight and that he was on his way. As you can imagine it was not the response I wanted. He could at least sound as scared as I was. He calmed me down over a cup of tea and was and still is one of the few friends who did not judge me or the children.

Maddy was also diagnosed with dyslexia as well as ADHD when she was very young. She attended a school for special needs for two years and then proceeded to a mainstream school where she matriculated. She was hyperactive and also did not have many friends. Although she overcame the hyperactivity, she still has dyslexia and therefore, since high school, prefers to write in English, so that she can do a spelling check afterwards on the computer. This book is consequently written in English, although it is not our mother tongue.

As you can imagine Mario did not tell his friends about his gifts while he was still young. For example, he can feel (and sometimes see) the difference in the energy of a diamond and a crystal. Nobody believed him. They joked about it and Mario learned to keep quiet about his abilities.

When he was still at school, he started working for his own pocket money. Firstly, he started as a runner in a restaurant, then a waiter, then in a coffee bar and then as a barman in a restaurant making cocktails and drinks and loving it. After school he worked in Maine in the USA at a ski resort as a waiter. Back in South Africa, while he studied, he worked at a bar as a mixologist. He then worked as a restaurant manager, just after completing his studies as a photographer and video maker. From time to time he tried different jobs. He worked as a marketer, a film extra and a film cast coordinator. He was also a trapeze artist in a circus but became ill and could not continue. At the end of the day he always ended up working as a bartender. He trained the VVIP barmen for the soccer world cup in 2010 and helped new restaurants to set up their bars and trained their bartenders. This was what he knew and what he was good at. Then two friends asked him to help them open a bar in another town and offered him a partnership. He opened the bar and worked there for six months until the business was doing well. Thereafter he decided to open his own bar in Cape Town.

The strange thing was that every time he worked on a project in the bar industry, he would be stopped. A door would close in his face. For example, he was not fully paid for the training of the barmen for the World Cup. Despite all of this he continued working because it was his passion, even though the bar environment was a challenging place to work in because of his spiritual gifts.

He received funding from an investor to open his own up-market cocktail lounge. The opening night was spectacular and a huge success. Everything went well. But then, BANG! .... The door was closed again. There was a problem with the renting contract which did not allow him to keep the cocktail lounge open, due to incorrect zoning of the premises.

What is he going to do know? Work in the film industry again, which is only a part time job, with no guarantees?

'What would you really like to do if money is not a factor?' I one day asked Mario.

He thought for a moment and answered, 'I would like to help and teach people spiritually. I think I finally got the message that God does not want me to work in a bar, but how do I begin? Where do I start? Do I pack a bag and walk out of the door? Where would I go mum? I do not know where to begin!'

I told him that it was a start to at least know what his real passion was. Mario then started counselling people spiritually, without charging a fee because at the time he believed that it is not right to ask for payment when he uses his gifts to work for God. He soon realized that working for free did not put bread on the table and he continued working in the film industry. He also decided that it was time to openly talk about his gifts to the people who wanted to listen. This was about the same time that I decided to write this book.

I have mentioned that Maddy is the flipside of the coin. She also did not talk about her gifts and still does not. I get the impression that she wants to forget about it. Although she can see (and feel) the difference between the energy of a diamond and a crystal for instance, she would not tell you, even if you asked. I remember when she was still young and we were strolling along the market place in our town. People with jewellery stalls would tell us to come and look at their crystal jewellery and she would tell me,

'Don't bother mum. It is glass or plastic. They are lying.'

As she became older she started closing up and became silent most of the time. Gone was the spontaneous hyperactive little girl and in her place was this shy adult. I knew that she was afraid to talk about her gifts. But I did not know what was going on in her head.

Sometimes Mario, Maddy and I would sit in my living room and talk about their gifts and the spiritual world. Then I always felt so sad that the inside of this room is the only safe place for us to talk freely and openly about everything, without being judged. However, Maddy did not even want to talk about her gifts with us anymore.

Maddy always wanted to work with animals. She practised horse riding as a hobby since the age of seven. While we were living at the coast she would look after people's dogs when the owners were away on holiday. During school holidays she worked at dog kennels and horse stables. After school she worked and studied for a month on a horse farm. She then continued her studies and became a qualified game ranger and field guide.

After completing her studies, she worked at a lion farm but decided to leave because of certain circumstances. It broke her hart to leave the lions, especially a weak little cub which she protected from his stronger siblings and nursed until he was stronger.

She then worked as an au pair and got a position at an organic nursery and doggie crèche. There she cleaned, washed, scrubbed, polished, planted, digged, painted and worked herself to the ground for a small token. Needless to say, she had not told her employer about her gifts.

Eventually she landed her dream job, although it did not pay much. She became a horse trail guide in the southern suburbs of Cape Town. She took tourists on horseback along the sea in a nature reserve. Some days she had three shifts and would be on horseback for six hours, apart from saddling the horses before the trails and grooming and feeding them thereafter. She worked hard, but loved every moment of it. She still walked dogs and did house sitting for dog owners in her free time, until she was offered a permanent position on the horse farm. While working on the farm, she studied part time and qualified herself as a stable manager as well as a horse riding instructor.

An interesting thing that happened during this time was that a lady whose two dogs were not behaving made an appointment with Maddy to communicate with her dogs. This was the first time she acknowledged her gifts to a stranger. When she told me about it, I was very happy but also surprised, because I did not know about the fact that she could communicate with them. When I asked her when she started to communicate with animals, she just answered that she could not remember.

'Do you talk to Minki (our cat) as well?' I asked, because I would have liked to know what Minki has to say for herself.

'No,' she answered.

'Why not?' I asked.

'Because she has an attitude,' she answered.

This was true, because Minki would decide when she would grace us with her presence and attention. I realised that because Minki was part of the family, she was too close to home for Maddy to feel comfortable to communicate with. She would rather communicate with animals of strangers, because she does not care so much if they judge her.

I wondered how I could help her to acknowledge her gifts and use them to help animals. This also prompted me to write this book. I talked to God and asked him to show me how to go about it. I also told Him that I would only do it, if both the children were positive and willing to help me with the book. After all, it was more their story than mine. I am just the mother who often wonders why I was blessed with these two gifted children. I prayed to God to help them to realise their potential and to see God's plan through writing this book together.

I bought three hardcover books and gave Mario and Maddy each one and kept the third one for myself. I wrote a number of similar topics in their books, which became most of the chapters of this book. Mario and Maddy wrote their stories independent of each other, without knowing what the other was saying. I did not want them to read each other's stories, because I did not want them to influence each other. In my book I wrote about my knowledge and experience of their gifts in order to fill in the blanks and to consolidate all the facts.

CHAPTER TWO
The vibrations of energy

I instructed Mario and Maddy to relax on their stoeps and close their eyes. They must then open their eyes and start writing about what they observe.

Mario started by writing, 'I am sitting on my stoep with closed eyes, wondering where to start. I open my eyes and look at the sky, thinking of how I always have seen things differently. When I look at the sky it looks like a slightly snowy picture on the television. I can see all the particles in the sky vibrating. This is how everything looks to me. Until my late teens I thought that everyone sees it in this way. When I found out that the world around me is not supposed to look like that, I went to an eye specialist for an eye test. He prescribed glasses and I thought that when I receive them, my eye sight would be fixed. Well, I could see road signs better, but the sky was still vibrating and moving. After misplacing my glasses after a year of wearing them, I did not bother to get a new pair. Some years later, I decided to have laser eye surgery. It was a success and my vision improved to 20/20, but the sky still moved! I then started focusing more on what I really see and came to realise that it was the particles making up the sky. I was amazed when I realised that I could see the vibrations of energy. Even with my eyes closed, I could still sense it.'

'I am a *clairsentient*. Most of you would probably think that you know what a *clairvoyant* is. It is not somebody who can see spirits and into the future. A *clairvoyant* is simply a person with the gift of sight who can see beyond the normal perception of man. They can see more vibrations that the human eye actually registers. A *clairsentient* is a person whose sense of touch or tactical feeling, is heightened to pick up energy and vibrations beyond what the normal sense of touch of man is supposed to be.'

'I feel everything! It is like a blind man whose other senses are heightened due to his loss of sight, but only much, much more, to the extent that I can feel the difference between real diamonds and fake ones. I can feel humans, animals, angels, demons, spirits and many more, without seeing them. That is why I prefer to walk at night without any light source. Light forces me to concentrate on my sight, instead of my tactile and proprioceptive senses. Without light I can focus better on all obstacles and move more freely.

'All of this is possible because of the vibration of energy! Simple physics!! Everything that exists in our world is made up of atoms which consist of a neutron and electrons. The electrons move around the neutrons. When clumped together it forms matter and still vibrates. A rock can lie perfectly still for years without moving, but the atoms are moving, giving off energy and vibrations. Thus, it is moving and perfectly still at the same time.'

'This constant vibration of energy gives off a certain frequency. This means that everything that exists has a specific frequency signature which gives off certain colours. By being able to pick up these vibrations or energy, I have come to recognise a lot of them through my tactical and proprioceptivesenses. This also helps me to distinguish between the frequency signature of solid matter, like a rock or person, as well as spirits, angels and demons. Proprioception is a sixth sense that has to do with balance, movement and spatial position of the muscles of the body. I am sure that most of you have also heard of a seventh sense, which is the vestibular sense that is centred in the inner ear and plays a role in balance while swinging, dancing, and the turning of the body.'

'Over the years I have created a way of visualising how my feelings look. This is how I can see in my mind's eye into the spiritual world by feeling the energy, vibrations and frequency signatures. Sometimes, when God needs me to focus on specific beings, He allows me to see it for real and that is how I know He is purposefully showing it to me. That is when I focus hard and zoom in to what is going on with the vibrations of energy around me. Because of this gift, everything can sometimes be too much and too overwhelming and I have learnt to sort of "turn it off", so that I do not become crazy. That said, there are some energy vibrations that I cannot turn off ......my guardian angels. Them, I can always feel and sometimes also see.'

When Maddy was about twelve years old, she was having more and more problems with her eyes. They were very sensitive to light and she was always rubbing her eyes, especially when outside. We made an appointment for an eye test and the optometrist told us that she had exceptionally large pupils, which were very rarely seen in humans. He also told us that her eyesight was excellent. In fact it was 100%, which means that no person on earth could have better eye sight than her. He advised us to get a pair of good sunglasses so protect her eyes from the light. I often wondered if this could be the explanation for her sensitivity to see energy in the physical, as well as the spiritual world, although I know it is a spiritual ability that she has.

While we were still living in our coastal town, Mario, Maddy and I were sitting and talking about a Reiki practitioner I had met. While we were talking about healing and energy, Maddy suddenly told us that her hands and arms looked the colour of indigo. She then looked at Mario and told him that he had an indigo light all around him as well. Mario could also see this and they told me that I have a pink colour shining around me. I believe this was the first time that they both could see the colours of energy, or auras, as it is more commonly known. I told them then what I knew about Indigo children, as I came across this information while I was studying for my Master Degree in play therapy. During the last 30 odd years, more and more babies were born with indigo auras. Indigo children are more intuitively and spiritually inclined and the colour of the energy around them (auras) is mostly indigo, a dark purple-blue colour. Indigos are often wrongly labelled as children with ADHD or learning disorders. Although a person's aura is mostly a specific colour, it can change from time to time, as the energy of the emotions and health changes. The primary colour would stay the same. Mario and Maddy's auras were indigo, and we could make the assumption that they were indigo children. They were so excited and ran to their father, who was watching television, and told him that he was orange. As you can imagine, he did not know what was going on and told them to stop their nonsense.

That was the time when Maddy started to climb onto the roof of our house to watch the power lines, which in those days were still up on poles, instead of underground. She could see the energy of the electricity flowing through the lines, almost like the readings of a heart monitor. She told me that she could see golden-yellow energy balls moving like little lightning bolts.

She also loved to sit there and watch all the colours of the energy around her. Some days when I was looking for her, she would be very high up in a tree in the neighbour's back yard. This was her time out, perhaps also her way of dealing with her hyperactivity that was still very much a part of her life. The most amazing thing was that she could sit like that for more than an hour at a time. Sometimes she would watch our Jack Russell dogs and then she would tell me that Foxie, for instance, was a bit orange or purple that day. She lived in a very colourful world. Mostly she did not want to talk about it, because she felt that she was used as a tool, if we put pressure on her to look at people's auras. She wanted to look in her own time and for her own reasons, without being pressed or judged by anybody.

When Maddy started her high school years at boarding school in Paarl, the window of her room had a beautiful view of Paarl Mountain and more specifically, Paarl Rock. For those of you who don't know Paarl Rock, I must explain that the radiation of this rock is quite extreme. One day, while she was sitting on her bed looking out of the window, she looked at the rock and couldn't believe her eyes. The energy radiating out of the rock and up in the sky was all the colours of the rainbow. While the colours moved and flowed upwards, it seemed endless and reached as far as her eyes could see. From that day on, it became her new past time, watching the colours of many rainbows, as she described it, reaching up into heaven. When she now has the time to drive past the rock, she always finds herself wishing that everybody could see this beautiful picture.

Maddy told me that when she feels an energy source, it is like when someone is entering a room and one can feel the presence before seeing it. Sometimes it would just feel as if someone is watching her. She can feel the moment the energy in the air around her changes. She then has to concentrate on the source to see the energy. If there is a lot of energy around, for instance in a crowd of people with all their guardian angels, she can distance her mind from it by blocking it out, otherwise it could be very overwhelming and tiring. For a very long time she chose to just block everything out, because she was afraid and did not know why she had this gift or how to handle it.

CHAPTER THREE
The spiritual world

Before I continue, I would like to give you my interpretation of the spiritual world. The Bible tells us about a fight that is not physical but indeed spiritual in Ephesians 6 verse 12:*"This is not a wrestling match against a human opponent. We are wrestling with rulers, authorities, the powers who govern this world of darkness, and spiritual forces that control evil in the heavenly world."*

Although we can see the physical world we live in, we normally cannot see the spiritual world. However, it is important to know that we live in both the physical and spiritual worlds. The spiritual world is amongst us in the "open spaces" we walk and talk and live in. The spiritual world is not far away or above us or only in heaven. It is around us and we are in it every day. This means that amongst us are spirits like angels and demons. We normally cannot see this world because the light energy contained in the atoms of people and objects in the physical world, is different from the light energy of the atoms in the spiritual world.

The Bible also tells us that sometimes God would let people of the physical world see into the spiritual world. Mary, for instance, saw an angel who brought her the message of her unborn child, Jesus, who would be born and Balaam, who was riding on his donkey, saw the angel of the Lord standing in his way.

Mario and Maddy have the gifts of feeling, hearing, knowing and seeing the energy in the physical, as well as the spiritual world. They also have the ability to zoom in on the energy by concentrating to do so. Why God has given them this ability, I do not know. What I do know is that God wants them to use these gifts to do well to others. How they must accomplish this, I also do not know. I do know that Mario wants to help people spiritually and Maddy wants to help animals and nature. I am praying every day that God will show them in His time, how they should use their gifts. As you can imagine, we are waiting eagerly for God to reveal His plan.

The big difference between Mario's and Maddy's gifts is that Mario can feel energy. When he really concentrates he can also see it in his mind's eye. The opposite is true for Maddy. She can see the energy and when she concentrates very hard, she can also feel it. She can also communicate with animals. Maddy explained to me that being able to see energy is a big deal for her. She would know it is there, but must focus and decide to look at it closely. In the beginning it was a very bad feeling, because she was afraid of what she would see.

The first time Maddy saw a spirit, which was not an angel or demon, was during a rainy winter's night. She told me the next morning that sometime during the night she woke up with the feeling that someone was in her room. Her hair stood on end and she sat up to look around. She then saw a little boy sleeping on the green beanbag in the corner of her room. He was curled up under her small television blanket. She was shocked and thought she was still asleep. She concentrated hard and could sense that he meant no harm. When she asked him why he was sleeping in her room, he answered that he was just resting in this comfortable and warm place for a while. By that time Maddy was not scared anymore and calmly wished him goodnight. After that she would tell me from time to time that he paid her a visit again during the night, especially on cold nights. He would just smile at her and go to sleep.

When I asked Mario about the spiritual realm he told me the following:

'As I started to understand more of the spiritual world, I learned very valuable lessons. Whenever I come across spiritual beings, I communicate with them through my senses and firstly ask them if they are from the darkness or the light. The next thing I always ask is what they are called by man. Lastly I ask them if they want to do me any harm. Then I decide whether I want them in my presence or to communicate any further. '

'Currently I find that there is a tremendous hype about aliens and whether the angels whom are spoken of in the Bible, were not simply alien encounters, described by simple folk as Godly or angelic. This then leads to the question that, if the beings my sister and I can sense and communicate with and perceive as angels, are in fact not aliens.'

'My answer is as follows: The beings we sense are very powerful creatures that exist with us, but vibrate with frequencies that are normally beyond man's normal senses. They are not from this planet and can go anywhere in the universe. They communicate by means that man normally cannot understand. They have wings and can fly and they can change their features within a split second. They are far more evolved than mankind and cannot be killed by our weapons.'

'Are they aliens? On this planet they are, yes. Are they UFO's? They are flying objects and mostly not identified or even seen by man, yes. Are they from another planet? No. They are from God. So, in retrospect I can understand that some people would like to believe that angels are aliens, and they would be partly right. All I can say is the beings that I know as angels are the same beings that Mary saw, that Jesus knew and that spoke to Ezekiel. They are the same beings that I communicate with and who protect me on a daily basis. This book is not about the rest of the aliens that may or may not be in the universe, but it is about the aliens I call angels.'

*Scripture is taken from GOD'S WORD®, © 1995 God's Word to the Nations. Used by permission of Baker Publishing Group.

CHAPTER FOUR
What do angels look like?

When Mario was still a little boy I realized that he was different in many ways from other little boys of the same age. For instance, he could move around in the dark at night without a torch or any other light source. It was as if he could feel his way through the darkness. He once told me that the moon was shining through his window every night on his bed, with the result that he could open his eyes during the night and see everything perfectly in his room. I told him then that it could not be the moon, because it could not be seen from that side of the house and suggested that it must be a light from the neighbours. We investigated this and realized that there were no streetlights or any other lights that could shine through his window, because there was no street at the back of the house and the wall was too high for the neighbours' lights to shine through his window. I thought that he was imagining things and forgot about it.

When he was older and became more spiritual, he realized that he has developed a way to see, by feeling like a blind person without his eyes. He then realised this ability was a gift to help him on his spiritual path. He could see by feeling things that were not visible in the physical world. He became aware of the energy of vibrations around him, energy that he came to know as angels, demons and other spiritual beings. When I asked him what angels look like, he explained to me as follows:

'I can describe how angels look, by feeling their vibrations. They normally look just like humans. Each one is different, like us, with a head, arms, body, legs, etc. The only difference is that most have wings or wing-like features that are used as shields and for flying. Sometimes they use them to emphasize their presence or power. They always appear in whatever form we find least fearful. They can be male or female. Most angels are huge in stature, but some can be the size of an average human person. Angels also have a set hierarchy. There are angels that have more authority than others, but believe it or not, there are humans that have higher authority than some angels.'

Mario also told me the following: 'Besides their similarities I see angels as faceless beings because I feel where their unique energy radiates from, instead of seeing their faces. Each angel has a unique energy signature which makes it possible for me to distinguish between them and 'see' where each one of them is. Sometimes though, when there is a legion of angels, their numbers are so vast, that I can only see where the group is.'

'One of my most memorable encounters with an angel that I will never forget happened after my dad died. That specific night, while sleeping in my bed, I briefly opened my eyes as I was turning around, and could not believe my eyes. I was immediately awakened by the sight I saw. Standing next to my bed was a figure with the head of a lion and an upper body like a well-built man. His lower body was wrapped in white cloths. He had four wings of which two were covering his legs and feet. I closed my eyes and opened them again to make sure that I was seeing what I believed I saw. I was a little bit scared and did not try to communicate with this vision. I closed my eyes for a few minutes and when I opened them again the vision was gone. The next morning I was still puzzled about what I had seen. At first I thought perhaps it was my dad whose name meant *lion*, but then I paged through a book with wonderful pictures and descriptions of angels, and to my amazement, I saw a drawing of the exact same picture that resembles the vision I saw that night. When I told my mum about it, she told me to read about the cherubs in the book of Ezekiel in the Bible. It was then that I realised it was not a vision of Dad, but a cherubim that visited me that night. I still wondered why he visited me, because according to the book I found on angels, I know that cherubims are usually in heaven around God and seldom seen on earth.'

Maddy describes angels as follows, 'They have big human-like bodies and the only real difference is their wings. The wings are very similar to what one sees in some of the movies. Their wings are large and cover their entire length. They look like feathers with a shine to it and are very, very soft and fluffy. They do not always spread their wings open, but sometimes just tuck them in neatly behind them. From time to time they will open them up for a stretch and tuck them in again. They only fly when they have to. When they are at my side they prefer to walk. I very rarely see them fly.'

'In the beginning, when I just started seeing them, I was still a little bit afraid and asked them to keep their distance, which they did with utmost respect. Later, when I was more used to them, I invited them to come nearer and I started communicating with them.'

The interesting thing about them that I realised only recently is that they do not have coloured auras like humans. They have a shiny silver, white and golden glow, which actually makes a lot of sense, as those are the colours of divine light. Angels do not have the problems, emotions and illnesses of humans who are still growing and striving to be divine and at peace.

'Angels also have different personalities, like humans. They can have all the good qualities of humans like being funny, friendly, loving and caring. They are not mean and will always speak the truth. They always respect my wishes and would never force me to do something I don't want to do. They would also never act against my wishes.'

'The choir angels are a little bit smaller and also radiate a bright silver and golden light. I normally see them in church, hospitals or at gatherings and ceremonies, like weddings and funerals. They always smile while they are singing. Once while I was in church, I closed my eyes and lifted my hands to praise and worship God. When I opened my eyes the whole ceiling was covered with angels, singing and dancing. I could see beams of bright white, silver and golden light shining from them. It was one of the most beautiful things I have ever seen or heard. I then realised how blessed I was with this most amazing gift, although I still do not know why.'

CHAPTER FIVE
Guardian Angels

When Mario was a young boy, he encountered many situations where he was in danger to the point where he could have died or been seriously injured, but he always walked away alive and well. Once he was hit by a car driven by thieves who tried to escape. He was thrown up into the air and landed on the pavement a meter away, unharmed and with only a scratch on his ankle. Not even concussion! When he was at pre-school, he fell backwards off a jungle gym onto a cement path, without any injuries. Later, when he was in his twenties, he was riding with friends on a mountain road when they suddenly saw a tree lying in the road. The driver tried to avoid the tree, spinning the car and crashing into a big tree standing next to the road. The car went up into flames and burnt out until only the frame was left. A friend, who was sitting at the back, was flown through the rear window about five metres away. He was unconscious with deep cuts in his face. The driver cut his arms and head with the glass of the window, while he escaped from the burning car and also had memory loss of the accident afterwards. Mario was in the flaming car with the door and window stuck. He escaped through the flames, through the broken window on the driver's side. He had only a little mark on his hip where the seatbelt nipped him.

Afterwards he told me, 'My guardian angels helped me.'

When I asked him about them he told me that in his experience most people are born with two guardian angels. Some people even have three.

This is what he told me, 'I have three guardian angels. I do not know their names. Their purpose is the same as the purpose of all guardian angels. God gave us all guardian angels and commanded them to guard, protect and help us, hence the title guardian angels. However, it is up to us to use them for that purpose. Angels do not have the gift of free will like us, they simply respond to commands given by a higher authority than theirs. God has also given each of us authority to talk to them and to ask them to help us with specific problems and in specific circumstances. With that said, let me introduce you to my guardian angels.'

'The first one is what I would call my body guard and bouncer. He is big and strong and very intimidating! He is the one whom I ask to protect me personally, my car, my house and any space that I need protected and kept safe. He always leans forward and places his arms around the space and then folds his wings around it all. He is also the one who always stands behind me, to help with his presence, to reinforce my authority in the spiritual, as well as the physical world.'

My second guardian angel is like a best friend. He is smaller in stature and he is the one I communicate with to ask for advice. If I feel lonely, he often gives me a hug to remind me that he is always there for me. He is always at my side.'

My third guardian angel is a female. In my experience I don't often come across female guardian angels. She is my conscience and helps me to remain in touch with my emotional side. She helps me to stay calm and also to distinguish between truths and lies.'

'When I am spiritually attacked, all three my guardian angels will take a fighting stance around me, just outside my bubble or personal space, ready to fight. When they need to, they will even grow in size to make a statement. I am almost always aware of them by feeling their energy and seeing them in my mind's eye. I communicate with them through my thoughts and emotions.

―――― ⚯ ――――

When Maddy was still in boarding school, she phoned me one night, sounding very strange.

'Mum I am scared. I am standing outside and there is an angel behind me. What must I do?'

'Talk to him and ask him what he wants," I told her.

'No, I am too scared,' she cried.

'Then run away,' I urged her tongue in the cheek, not really knowing what to believe.

Then she cried again over the phone, 'I tried, but he kept following me.'

I then told her to go inside were she would feel safe and talk to God about it'.

I phoned Mario and told him about her phone call and he phoned her to calm her down and to tell her what to do. She later told me it was the first one of her guardian angels that she could see.

On another occasion Maddy walked into my room one morning and sat on my bed while I was having my morning tea. She told me,

'Mum, you know about my three guardian angels that are always with me...,'

No, I do not know about them, I thought but just nodded.

'Well, when I go into a church, why is it that two of them always stay outside at the doors and only one follows me inside?' she asked.

'You have three guardian angels?' I asked.'

'Yes, of course, you know this mum,' she answered.

'No I do not know this, and how many guardian angels do I have?' I asked.

'You have two,' she answered.

'I did not know about my guardian angels because nobody told me about them,' I replied. 'But to answer your question, I think that the two angels stay at the doors outside to keep watch while the third one guards you inside. But why do I have only two guardian angels and you have three?' I asked.

'Because you only need two,' she answered and walked away.

Apparently people, who need more spiritual protection, have more guardian angels.

And that was how I found out about my two guardian angels. I am still planning to ask her what their names are and what they look like, but know that I must wait till the time is right and she is willing to talk about them again.

When we started writing this book, Maddy told me more about her guardian angels. She described them as follow, 'One of my guardian angels, the first one that I saw that night when I phoned you, is almost glued to my side. He follows me everywhere and stays by my side, no matter what. He is my bodyguard and will even sit on my bed when I go to sleep. He is very strong and his name is Emanuel. He has big, dark blue wings and beautiful blue eyes.'

'The second one's name is Zavior. He has a tremendous sense of humour and can be quite funny. He is not as close by my side as Emanuel and will rather stand by a window or patrol the house. He is very good with giving me advice, but is also a very important link in my protection system. He is the size of an average human male with creamy coloured wings and big brown eyes.'

'Elisha is my life coach and is also always nearby. She is very upfront and personal and tuned into my emotions and thoughts. She is calm and peaceful and is always smiling. She is the one that is helpful and comforting when I have a problem. She has the most amazing white-pink wings, dark brown hair and blue eyes. They all have a very personal relationship with me, unlike the rest of the angels who communicate with me from time to time and then go their merry way to do whatever they have to do. I seldom call my guardian angels by their names, because they are so in sync with me and know my thoughts at once, even before I communicate with them. They know when I am talking to one of them specifically, or to all of them together. They are my friends and I cannot imagine life without them.'

'I am becoming more aware of my guardian angels lately and a few days ago a funny thing happened while I was driving alone in the rain. I zoomed in to see where my guardian angels were and saw that while Emanuel was with me in the car, Elisha and Zavior were flying next to my car, one on either side. While the soft rain was drizzling down, the two angels were playing some kind of game. They were flying, looking to see which one of them could stay the closest to the side of my car, while still focusing on me to see if I was safe. I decided to play along and slowed the car down before quickly moving to the fast lane and speeding up again. They laughed at me and warned me to be careful and to watch what I was doing. When the rain came down faster and harder, they decided to stop the game and got into the car. It is always amazing how they fit into a small space like my car, with their big bodies, without sitting on each other.'

'Another time, the two guys were flying next to my car, while Elisha was taking control of my steering wheel, to protect me and guide me to prevent an accident. It was so cool, they all literally guided me out of the situation. Although I have never been in an accident with my car, it has minor bumps and scratches for which I was responsible. Perhaps they allowed the minor damage to show me that I am not invincible on the road and still have to be very careful, in spite of their presence.'

One night, while I was watching television, Maddy asked me,

'Mum, do you know the names of your guardian angels?'

'No, I do not, but I would like to know',

'I have communicated with them, something I never did before, and written about them and can tell you their names and how they look, if you want me to', she told me.

'That would be so cool', I answered.'

'I already told you that you have two guardian angels, one male and one female. The male is big and strong with dark hair, hazel eyes and dark wings. His name is Luan and he is very tall, dark and handsome. He is your body guard and acts quickly and moves fluently. With you, he is like a gentle giant. Then there is Cassidy. She is the one that is always very close to you. She is like a beam of sunshine in your life, with a great sense of humour. She has light toffee coloured hair with green eyes and big white and cream wings.'

'Wow, thank you for telling me. It makes me feel safe and happy', I thanked her.

'No problem, you are welcome', she answered and off she went again.

CHAPTER SIX
Accidents and bad things still happen

It is important to realise that in spite of seeing angels and knowing our guardian angels are watching over us, accidents and bad things can still happen to us. It is the same as believing in God and still being poor or ill. We still have free will and can make our own choices. Believing in God and angels is not going to secure a blissful life. Our guardian angels are not going to stop us from making our choices or behaving badly, only God can do that, although he usually allows us to make mistakes and hopefully learn from them. Apart from having free will, there are also many bad and evil people who want to do us harm. They will still steal, murder, lie, and do wrong to us in spite of God and the angels. That is why it is so important to pray and ask God to protect us from evil and to ask our guardian angels to guard over us. Whenever I hear about an accident over the radio, I instantly ask God to send angels to the accident scene, as well as to the loved ones of the people who was involved in the accident, because I know how traumatic it could be for everybody.

I have related some accidents in which Mario was involved without him being injured. It is my firm belief that at those times his guardian angels watched over him and protected him. When he was in the rugby team in high school, however, he was also injured from time to time, but there was one accident in which he was very badly hurt. Although, I truly believe that if God and the angels were not there, it could even have been much worse. His head was hurt very badly, but he never lost consciousness. When the paramedics carried him from the field and into the ambulance and asked him what his address was, so that they would know to which hospital to take him, he gave the wrong address. He gave them our home address in Cape Town where we lived four years previously, before we moved to the coast. Luckily a friend could tell them the correct address, and they could take him to the right hospital. When he arrived at the hospital the coach called us. We rushed to the hospital where he was waiting in the emergency room for the results of the X-rays. After examining the X-rays, the doctor told us that there were no serious injuries and that he would only keep Mario in hospital over-night because he had sustained concussion.

The next morning when I arrived at the hospital, Mario told me that he had no idea why he was in the hospital. He could not remember what had happened. When he found out that he was in a hospital at the coast instead of Cape Town, he was even more confused. We talked about this for a long time and then realised that he had memory loss and could not remember the past four years since we had moved. This is known as selective amnesia and usually happens when the emotional part of the brain cannot deal with severe trauma. The doctor reassured us that this would pass in a day or two, but decided to keep him hospitalized until he regained his memory. After three days he was discharged, although he still had selective amnesia. The doctor told us that we had nothing to worry about and that he would soon start remembering. When we reached the parking lot of the hospital, he was very surprised to see my new car. Needless to say I had been driving the car for more than two years by then.

When his friends started visiting him at home, he could not remember them at all, not their names, faces or anything about them, not even his girlfriend! As you can imagine it was a big shock to all of them and a lot of them cried in disbelief because he did not remember them. Maddy and I spent a lot of time with him and spoke at length about various incidents and showed photos of the past four years, all of which he could not remember. We told him stories about his friends and girlfriend, but all in vain, his memory did not return.

We then made an appointment with a neurologist who referred him for a scan, but he could also not find anything wrong with Mario. The scan showed no signs of any brain damage which could cause the memory loss. After three weeks at home Mario decided to go back to school. The only problem then was that he did not remember anything about his school. One of his friends took him from class to class and introduced him to his teachers, told him where to sit and which books to open. This was very hard for him. Some of his class mates thought he was lying about the amnesia and made fun of him and joked about it. The hardest part was when we realised that Mario also had no memory of any of the school work he had done the past four years. This was a big shock. I arranged for extra classes in maths and science. I personally helped him at home with biology and languages. A friend helped him with computer science and he only had to do geography on his own. Everybody helped with the past four years' work, which he had totally forgotten.

He struggled to prepare for the end of that year's exams and we prepared ourselves for the possibility that he would not pass. Luckily he did and the next year, his last in high school, he was back to his own form and did very well and even won some awards for maths and culture.

Besides all the studying he still had to come to terms with his memory loss. There were still a lot of blank spaces that we had to fill in for him. To this day we do not know if he regained his memory, or if he just learned to live with the information and facts he found out from his family and friends.

During that year another strange thing happened one evening. He was working again at a coffee shop during weekends and holidays. One evening, while he was on his way home from work on his bike, a car almost ran him over. Although he fell, he was not really hurt, apart from a few scratches, but he had memory loss again. He drove on, but did not know where he was and where to go to. I was worried when it started getting dark and he had not returned home, but thought he had decided to wait for the rain to pass. Some hours later, I heard him at the back door. He walked straight to me and hugged me and cried for a long time and then told me,

'I did not know where to find our house and drove in circles for hours. All I knew was that I must stay near the sea. When I saw the house, I just turned in without knowing why. It was only a feeling I had and cannot explain it at all. Maybe it was an angel?'

That night his dad slept in the same room with him to make sure that he was okay. The next morning he could not remember anything of the previous night. When we told him about it, he was shocked and surprised, but also worried that he would lose his memory again. Although I phoned the neurologist to tell him about this episode, he could not give us an explanation. Since no brain damage showed on the scan, he could not do anything for. I experienced a profound sense of sadness that while he was going through this very difficult time in his life, only his nearest family and close friends cared.

When Mario decided to go to work in the USA at a ski resort the following year, we were very worried that he would lose his memory again. For Christmas we gave him a silver chain with his name, address and telephone number to wear. Luckily everything went well and no incident like this happened again.

One rainy winter's morning when Maddy was on her way to school a terrible thing happened to her. We lived in a complex nearby, just next to the school. She only had to walk through the entrance of the complex, around the corner and over the street at the zebra crossing to reach the school. That particular morning she left earlier than usual to help a friend with some school work. It was still dark and while she was walking over the street at the zebra crossing, she suddenly saw the lights of an oncoming car. She found it very strange because she was always very careful and always looked left and right before crossing the street. She then thought to herself that the car must still be far away and she would be fine because she was almost at the other side. The next moment the car hit her and she was thrown up into the air and landed three meters back in the street, right in the way of the oncoming traffic. Everything happened very fast. Another person who was driving past and did not see her in time also hit her with the cars wheels. Maddy could feel that the wheel of the car connected with her and shifted her nearer to the pavement.

While she was lying in the road in the rain, she thought that she had lost her leg because of the terrible pain she was feeling. Everybody rushed to her side, starting to talk and scream. She told them to phone Mario on her cell phone which was lying nearby in the road. Then she shut all her senses down because she could not bear to hear, see, smell and feel the pain and trauma. Although she was still conscious, her survival mode kicked in and she concentrated on singing a song in her head. The next thing she was aware of again, was Mario touching her and talking to her. Although she was relieved that he was there, she then began to feel the pain again, as well as the rain and the hard tar road at her back. Everybody was standing with umbrellas over her, but the rain dripped down the sides onto her face and body. The first thing that came to her mind was who would pay the doctors' bills and what was going to happen at school.

While she was still lying in the road, waiting for the ambulance, the traffic police cordoned off the road for the oncoming traffic and the cars had to pass on the pavement. My brother-in-law drove past looking at the girl lying in the street and felt very sorry for her. He was looking at the contrast of her one white hand on the black road in the rain, without knowing it was her. Eventually the ambulance arrived and the school left a message for me at my work place that Maddy had been in an accident. I had just reached my work place that morning and promptly made a U-turn and started driving back from Stellenbosch to Durbanville in the heavy rain.

Her suitcase was totally destroyed in the accident and it looked as if it had been in an explosion. Only Maddy's stockings were torn and there was no further damage to her school uniform. Maddy's knee, where the car hit her, was very badly hurt and she needed an operation. The doctor was also concerned that she could have back and neck injuries. Fortunately her back and neck were fine, which the doctor told us was a miracle. He warned us that her whole body would be very sore with lots of bruises during the course of the next few weeks. To the doctor's amazement, she was not bruised or sore at all. Two days later, because there was no operating theatre available sooner, she had the operation on her knee. While we were waiting in the waiting room, Mario told me that he saw the doctor's as well as the rest of the staff's guardian angels, when he accompanied Maddy to the operating theatre.

During the course of the day of the accident, a teacher phoned me to apologise for "driving over" Maddy. At the time I did not know what she was talking about, as Maddy showed no injuries as evidence. I asked Maddy about this, and she answered that she could remember something bumping her and shifting her nearer to the pavement. I asked the doctor to check it out, but he said that her only injury was her severely damaged knee. I did not understand what was going on, but for a split second got a picture in my mind of an angel catching Maddy and softly putting her down next to the pavement. Later Maddy told me that was exactly how it felt at the time.

An interesting fact was that the man who was responsible for the accident profoundly apologized at the accident scene and told Maddy over and over that he was very sorry and that it was his fault. The next day, however, he phoned me and told me that he was the owner of the vehicle that Maddy walked into without looking, and he emphasized that she was responsible for it. That was the last time we heard anything from him, as the police took over the case. The traffic department and our lawyer found that he was indeed responsible and told us that we could press charges, but we decided against it. All that mattered to us was the fact that Maddy was well, although she had some hardware in her knee and I am only thankful to God and the angels for whatever they did that day to help her.

After eight weeks Maddy returned to school. While she was at home, nobody except family contacted us, not even once to find out how she was or when she would be returning school. It felt like a repetition of when Mario had his accident playing rugby.

When she returned to school she was afraid to cross the street at the zebra crossing and started to cross it at a stop sign, which was very dangerous for pedestrians during peak times. It was then that she decided to apply for the boarding school where her best friend from primary school was in residence.

CHAPTER SEVEN
The worst things in life

According to research the most difficult things to handle in life are: (1) the death of a loved one, then (2) divorce, then (3) a severe accident or losing a limb or having a terminal illness, then (4) moving to another town. Mario and Maddy experienced all four in a period of two years.

When their father and I were divorced, we had to move from our lovely five bedroom home at the sea, to a small two bedroom apartment in a complex in Cape Town, because I had to find employment and my chances were better in the city. Wow, we felt like fish being scooped from the ocean and put into a small fish bowl! Maddy had to start high school and left all her lifelong friends behind. This was at a stage when friends were very important to her. She also had to share a room in our little apartment and lost some of her privacy, which was a big deal for a teenager. She hated the new school and had no friends. All her class mates had known their friends for years and did not bother to make friends with this shy girl whose parents were going through a divorce. She really tried very hard to fit in, but then I realised that she was only making herself believe that she was fine, which she was not. She was a soft target for her class mates to be mean to her and they would for instance put a notice on her back with the words "kick me" or "I am an arse-hole".

Before we moved to Cape Town, Mario was studying there, but he also missed our house, the sea and mountain and his friends as much as the rest of us. Of course, he also missed his dad. Then his high school sweetheart, his girlfriend for five years, ended their relationship. He told me at the time that it felt as if he was going through his own 'divorce'.

The upheaval was very hard on everybody, but the worst thing was that we decided to have our two dogs, our pets for seven years, euthanized. We were not allowed to keep any pets in our apartment. We tried to find a new home for them, without any success. We kept them secretly in our small backyard for three days, but soon the secret was out and our landlord threatened to evict us if we did not get rid of them. At last we found a farmer who was willing to take them, but he warned us that if they gave him or the farm animals any trouble, he would shoot them. That was when we decided to let them go. It was the hardest decision I have ever made in my life and I am still sorry about it. We had already lost so much. I hated the neighbours who complained about the dogs and reported us. We grieved for our dogs for a very long time.

Through all this drama, my sister, their aunt, had terminal cancer and was fighting for her life. She was diagnosed four years previously and would continue fighting for four years to come. Together with her husband and son we were fighting the cancer with her and were part of the ups and downs, the good news and bad news, the hope and despair.

Then the children's dad died. Two years after the divorce he died of a heart condition he suffered from for a very long time. We were just getting used to being without him, and then he died on us. I often secretly wished that he had died before the divorce, to spare the children the pain of losing him twice.

One Sunday afternoon Maddy and I were sitting on my stoep, eating water melon. I told her about her uncle, the doctor, who believed it is bad for the appendix to swallow the pips. We joked about this and kept eating our water melon with pips and all. Later that day I started feeling ill. I had a severe ache in my abdomen. I tried some medicine, but it did not help at all. The pain was so severe that I called my brother-in-law, the doctor, who came to my house and told me he thought it was my appendix. It was indeed my appendix and the joke was on me.

He and my sister rushed me to hospital. When we arrived at the hospital they put me in a wheelchair, because the pain was so agonizing that I could not walk. They pushed me into the elevator to go to the ward and believe it or not, we got stuck between two floors. There we were, me doubled over in the wheelchair because of a burst appendix, a fact we did not know at the time. My brother-in-law was on his cell phone trying to arrange assistance on this late Sunday evening and my sister getting tired of holding on to me, because she was afraid I would fall out of the wheelchair. She was very sick at the time due to her chemotherapy. We were stuck like this for more than an hour. When we eventually got to the ward, I was told that they could do nothing for me except to give me medication for the pain, because it was Sunday. I was operated on the next evening at ten o'clock, because there were no theatres available earlier in the day. I waited for more than 24 hours and as you probably know, no pain medication helped at all for a burst appendix.

Mario has started a new job some months earlier at a company that was supposedly going to train him as a marketing manager. They flew him with stars in his eyes, in style to Johannesburg. When he got there, he was trained as a marketer with other candidates. Then they were told that the first step, just to get them going, was to do door-to-door sales. So, during the days they were trained and in the evenings they were dropped off in neighbourhoods, knocking on doors for four hours every evening, and then were picked up again.

During my stay in hospital, while he was getting ready for the evening's job, Mario was stung by a scorpion in the shower. He was taken to hospital, where the doctor gave him a lot of medication. When I phoned him that evening from my hospital bed, he was delusional and could not speak to me coherently. He was not sure of the day or the time. He told me that he passed out for a while and was waiting for the others to get back. The next morning, after many phone calls, I arranged for someone to take him to a nearby town to catch a bus home. He made his way there with his suitcase and the clothes on his back, but did not have any money for the bus fare. He then found out that the bus pickup was in another town some forty kilometers away. There he was, a stranger in the middle of a strange little town, feeling delirious, without any money or transport. He managed to get to a B&B with the name of Lavender Lane and asked the owner for some help. He told him about his situation and that he had no money. This gentleman let him stay for the night, gave him breakfast and took him to the bus stop the next day. I still think of him as one of the 'human angels on earth' that crossed our path. He made me realize that there were still a lot of good and kind people.

During this time Maddy was home alone and to put the cherry on the cake, she got 'dumped'. She was dating a very nice young man whose father was a doctor. When the parents found out that their son was dating for the first time, they insisted that she meet the parents, by inviting her on a weekend hiking trip. At the time I wondered if this was a test but kept my thoughts to myself. When I contacted the mother I told her that I was concerned about Maddy's knee, because it was still weak, but she assured me that her husband was a doctor and would handle any problems. I wondered at the time how he was going to handle it, for instance, if she hurt her knee again. Was he going to operate in the mountains or carry her down on his back?

They went on the hiking trip into the mountains, but it did not go very well. After a few hours Maddy's knee was hurting and she could not keep up the pace. Her boyfriend offered to carry her backpack and he and a friend took turns to do so. That helped a lot, and although she was at the back of the group, she made it that day. Needless to say, they did not get to meet Maddy at her best. This was the girl and nature lover who had been camping from the day she could walk and who would become a game ranger and horse trail guide, not keeping up. Things did not work out and due to peer pressure and outside forces they broke up and the next weekend was the Sunday of the water melon pips episode.

While I was in hospital and Mario on the bus on his way home, Maddy was all on her own, heartbroken and very much afraid that one of us would die. Luckily we all survived this double ordeal.

When I look back at those times, I cannot believe that we came through it all. I often wonder why Mario and Maddy had to cope with double, or even triple the problems and pain that most young people of their age can't even begin to imagine. When I voiced this question one day, Mario answered,

'It is God's way to make us stronger.'

'How much stronger does God want us to be?' I wondered aloud.

'As strong as Samson of the Bible? Why do we have to be so strong?'

'Because He wants us to be strong to do what we have to do for Him when the time comes."

'To do what?'

'Be patient mum,' the wise one told me.

And that is how I survived all this. My children and my faith in God were, and still are, my inspiration to make lemonade from the lemons life gave me. I did not give up because of them, but also for them. I did not despair. How could I, by knowing that my guardian angels put their wings around me to embrace me. What a wonderful and peaceful thought to always remember.

My friends also played a big role in my survival by listening to me and being there for me. They were my counsellors and mentors, even if they did not know how big the role was that they were playing in my life at the time.

Luckily good things also happened. I got a permanent job at the college I was teaching at and could afford to buy my little 'fish bowl' I was renting at the time. The Road Accident Fund paid out the exact amount Maddy needed to study for a game ranger. She also had the opportunity to feed elephants, worked with lions, swam with dolphins and worked with horses. She met the love of her life and got engaged. Mario met his soulmate on a film set they were working on. She acknowledges his gifts and does not freak out when we talk about the spiritual world. They became engaged and are very happy together. Although I am still single, I am embracing life and live it to the fullest. One of my best experiences ever, was when one of my counsellor-mentor friends and I, were privileged to ride in a hot air balloon over Lake Bled in Slovenia. Wow, despite the hard times, life was and still is great …!

CHAPTER EIGHT
Demons, evil spirits and ghosts

One night, a few years ago, while I was getting ready for bed, I heard a strange noise outside my bedroom window. It was as if somebody was dragging a thick chain across the pebbles in my garden. The noise stopped under my window. I moved my curtains an inch and looked through the opening to see what it was, but I couldn't see anything. When I turned away, I heard the dragging sound go over my roof and stop at the guest bedroom's window on the other side of my house. I quickly, but softly, walked into the room and peeped out of the window, but still could not see anything. I then put on the light in the bedroom and opened the curtains wide. While I was doing this, I was also praying for protection, because I realised that this was a spiritual experience. I could only hear the sounds but could not see anything. The loud sounds of the dragging of the chain went over the roof again and stopped outside my bedroom window. I went to my room, put on the light and while openly looking out of the window, I phoned Mario and told him about it. While I was talking to Mario I could hear the sound moving through my garden and away from the house.

Although Mario was already in bed at his place, he told me that he was on his way and that I must stay calm and keep praying. Within ten minutes Mario arrived at my place. He told me that he could sense something evil when he entered at the gate of the complex, but he also could not see anything. He then walked around the house and told me that whatever it had been was gone, although he still could sense the energy that it left behind. It definitely was unfriendly and evil. He then anointed my house and decided to stay for the night.

We talked for a while and I then realised that sometimes during the night, I heard strange noises, which I could not explain. I learned that if Minki, our cat, became alert, it was not my imagination, because she could also hear it. So from that night on, I always look at Minki, to see if she is alert or not. If she is listening, I start praying to God and the angels for protection. When something like this happens, it amazes me that I am not scared at all, because I really trust in God and believe that he would not allow anything evil to happen to me.

Sometimes I detect a strange odour in my home, for instance, a strong whiff of an unknown perfume or aftershave, while watching television. Sometimes I smell food that I haven't cooked, like pancakes with cinnamon. I then go outside to smell who of my neighbours is making pancakes, but usually I am unable to find the source. I have made the assumption that I am able to smell and hear spiritual entities, but cannot see into the spiritual world, because I do not really want to. Although

I would love to see angels, I am definitely not ready to see evil spirits. I am sure that because God understands this, he protects me from seeing them.

I am sure that at some or other time all of you have heard of the law of attraction. In other words, what you send into the universe, you get back. This also goes with the law of fear, which is that what you fear you will attract. Then there is also the power of creation of words, where words are energy and become intent. Thus we must always be careful what words and energy and intent we put out into the universe. Just imagine what the words "damn you (to hell)" could do for a person. It just may come true. Imagine you say those words, accompanied by your fear of not directing it to yourself and then getting all that energy back. It's powerful stuff! But if you say for instance "bless you" it becomes energy and intent and can bless the person and yourself. Mario told me that angels, demons and spirits are all around us and have to follow the laws of the spiritual world. When communicating with a spirit, the first thing to find out is who the source is. Is it from the darkness or the light?

Keeping in mind that spirits vibrate at different frequencies to humans, they have difficulty vibrating in harmony in the same space as humans. The laws of the spiritual realm work automatically, whether we believe in it or not. It is not a matter of believing, but only of understanding it. The spiritual realm has lighter vibrations than our heavy 3D physical realm. In the spiritual world, energy manifests and exists faster and easier. When, for instance, we asks or visualise or imagine a legion of angels for protection around us, it is instantly real in the spiritual world.

So which kinds of spirits do we get in the spiritual world? The word *spirit* comes from the Latin word *spiritus* which means *breath*. This means that anything that has existence and consciousness but cannot be experienced in our definition of the material world is spirit. They are beings that vibrate with higher energy intensity than in our physical world.

It is also very important to know that ghosts are not spirits. Any encounter with ghosts will reveal that one cannot interact or communicate with them. It seems as if they go through the same motions over and over like being stuck in a loop. Normal protection against spirits does not work with ghosts. This is because ghosts are not real. Ghosts are simply messages. Mario explained them as follows:

'When a human experiences a traumatic event like the death of a loved one, it is even more traumatic if it is an unnatural or violent death. The person dying sends out a distress signal as the spirit leaves the body. This signal or message exists as energy in the area where the death occurs and can be intercepted by a human receiver. This is where the idea of ghosts 'haunting' a house or place comes from. As we all know, humans do not use their full potential and/or spiritual abilities and therefore our telepathic abilities are almost non-existent. However, we still have these abilities and can sharpen them. This is why a few of us can see ghosts and the rest cannot. Regardless, we struggle to receive or interpret the messages and usually receive distorted cries for help. Since energy cannot be destroyed, it lingers and we pick it up when we are in its presence. Ghosts can easily be removed by simply cleansing the energies in the area of ghost sightings.'

Mario told me that it is very important to know that demons and evil spirits do not have free will. They are only following orders from a higher being with higher authority. They can never take our lives without our permission, but can only evoke fear in us. Sometimes they can scare us so much, that we unknowingly give them permission to harm or even kill us. They can only use our own fear to succeed. The less afraid we are of them, the safer we are from them!

They use manipulation to scare us. They also scare us by the way our senses perceive or experience them. That is why they look like monsters and smell like rotten eggs and sulphur. That is also why they snarl and scream and speak with deep voices. These tactics are very effective because we are programmed with a flight or fight instinct and because some religions have taught us to believe we are weak and unworthy of power, most of the time we will take flight, unless we can justify ourselves to fight.

They can also manipulate energy in the physical realm. It is easy for them to move or destroy objects, manipulate the elements and even to create chemical reactions. Can you imagine how scary it would be if your cupboard doors fly open or your glasses shatter on the floor without a wind blowing or any other logical explanation? They can also physically harm you. They can scratch you, throw you on the floor or across the room or make your body react in strange ways. They can push you to the point where you wish you can just die and that is exactly what they want. This is why it is very dangerous to toy with demons and evils spirits, even if it is through the occult or from ignorance.

Luckily God gave us tools and methods to keep us safe from demons and evil spirits. Demons are essentially angels. They are angels whose commander, Samuel, the light bringer, gave them orders to lower their vibration, move down to earth and to adapt or be destroyed. Samuel now known to us as Lucifer. They were also told to evoke fear instead of love in humans. Their leader, known as Lucifer, gave them orders to take control of the physical world and to create the opposite of love, namely fear.

In heaven God has assigned specific jobs to all the archangels. Each archangel has his own legion of angels to assist with the different jobs. If you look at this through a military perspective, there is Lucifer, the general, and his warriors from the dark side and then there are all the other archangels with their soldiers, from the light. Keep in mind that we haven't even taken God into consideration when looking at this picture! As you can see, in the battle between the two sides, there can only be one winner – the light side. This doesn't mean that there would be no casualties on the light side, but it certainly means that the dark side is going to lose the battle between good and evil!

CHAPTER NINE
Healing

Mario is also a healer. When I asked him how it works, he explained to me as follows,

'The first time I tried to do healing, I put my hands without touching, palms down a few inches away, over a friend's body. I could feel a tingling sensation or soft vibration on the palms of my hands as I moved them. I could also feel heat coming from certain energy points in his body. I made my eyes softer without zooming in, with the result that my sight became out of focus. I then could sense multiple hands on mine, moving with mine, while there was a green glow around our hands. It felt as though these hands were helping me to sense the energy and to heal, by changing my friend's energy on that specific spot with my (our) hands. From that day, this light green colour became my colour of healing. Whenever I do healing now, I would close my eyes, still sensing the hands with the green glow on mine, while feeling the energy of the specific spot in the person's body, where my hands linger in the air above.'

'Over the years, I learned to distinguish between the differences in the temperature and frequency of the vibrations of the energy of different illnesses. I started to scan people by moving my hands slowly over their bodies, without touching them. I can sense if there are problems with certain organs, muscles, the skeleton or any other part of the body. I am also able to sense if there are emotional or spiritual blockages. By knowing that, I can proceed with the healing. I then ask God to send His healing light through me and to do His healing. I would visualise the healing and would immediately feel a vibrating warm sensation in the middle of my chest. I then visualise this green healing energy moving from my chest, down my arms and through my hands. At this point I feel the energy flowing out of my palms and into the body of the person. I then ask God to heal in whichever way he sees fit and then allow and trust the energy to flow freely.'

'Healing somebody in this manner is a two way street. Once the energy connection has been made, I also receive healing energy back. However, this exchange of energy can be dangerous. When I started healing people, I used to take their ailments onto myself. I would for instance take somebody's headache away by taking the energy into myself. The person's headache would be better, but I would have it myself in exchange. Another time, I tried to help a lady friend with her monthly pains. Let me tell you, it was no joke. While she was happy and smiling, I was experiencing pain on parts of me that I wasn't even supposed to have! I then realised that I must not use my own energy in this way. That was when I started to let God do the healing through me. Like in the saying, "Let God and let go." That's exactly how I do it now.'

'Through the years I realised that I could, for instance, feel the difference between a sprained or broken ankle. I also know the difference between inflammation and injury in a muscle and even between a malignant and benign syst.'

Maddy can do healing too. She can see the energy of people around them in colours. By looking at the different colours and change of colours, she knows were an ailment is. She can also feel it, if she puts her hands over, or on, it. She prefers to do healing on animals in this way. Of course she has the bonus of communicating with the animals. She would know, for instance, if a dog with cancer is in pain or not.

I have told you about the little lion cub she helped to get well and strong. She told me at the time that she thought he had lung problems. She sat with him on her lap every day, giving him some healing energy. She could sense that he was getting better and stronger as the days went by. When she left, she was satisfied that the little lion cub was healthy and strong enough to fend for himself.

CHAPTER TEN
Animal communication

Maddy enjoys working with animals, especially the last three years while she had mostly worked with horses. Her ability to communicate with them improved a lot and it became to her as natural as talking to people. She explained to me that animals are a lot like children.

'It is important to win their trust and respect first, before it is possible to communicate with them. But as it is with children, they do not necessarily listen to advice or commands. They can be very stubborn and sometimes choose not to communicate at all. Animals also have emotions and when they are fearful, uncertain, nervous, upset, angry or exited, it is difficult to get through to them and for them to focus on what I am trying to communicate to them. It is also difficult to communicate with them if they are hurt and in pain. Then they struggle to focus on what I am trying to communicate and will close up their minds, the same as children would do. I do not speak the words or whisper when I communicate. And of cause they do not bark or make their signature sounds when they communicate back. Everything happens in silence through our minds in a telepathic way. Although it is not unusual for me to speak the words and for them to make sounds when communicating, but this happens spontaneously without thinking about it, or being necessary.'

'After earning the animals' trust and respect, they must be in a relaxed and peaceful state of being. They must focus on the person who is communicating and wants to communicate. Only then communication is possible. The way in which I communicate depends on the type of animal. Through my experience I have learned that elephants, horses and dolphins are some of the most intelligent animals. They are more knowledgeable and I can 'speak' to them about topics like earth and nature. With them I can imagine a picture and ask them to look at the bigger scheme of things. With cats and dogs I communicate in a more basic way, although a lot of them are also very intelligent.'

'To animals the world does not matter. They are concerned in the here-and-know and want to survive and be content. The immediate things like their home, human families, food and love are important to them.'

'Not so long ago I was on my way to my garage, when I noticed dolphins in the waves. I walked straight to the beach to take a closer look. It was a school of dolphins swimming in different directions and I decided to communicate with them. Because they were so scattered, I found it very difficult because their minds were actively busy. I decided to walk into the water and then opened my mind and listened. I got bits and pieces and realized what all the excitement was about. They were hunting and herding the fish together. Then I saw them going very closely to the shark nets. I focused on one of them and warned him about the nets, but he communicated to me that they knew about it and that I don't have to worry. I then shifted my eyes to look at all the different energies and their happiness spread through me as I watched them. With the naked eye there wasn't much to see, only some fins breaching from time to time. But I could see and feel their happiness and excitement.

'I then realized again how lucky I was to have such an amazing gift. I promised myself then that I will use it with responsibility and care. I hope that people will allow me to share with them what I know. When people are willing to open their minds, there is space for so much more, which one cannot begin to imagine.'

EPILOGUE

Both Mario and Maddy are now happy with partners that support them whole heartedly, although their partners do not necessarily understand everything they do. I must confess that even I don't understand everything I have written about in this book, but as I explained in the beginning, this book was the platform for them to tell their stories and to feel more comfortable with whom they are.

As I am writing this epilogue there are large fires burning in the Southern Peninsula of Cape Town. Fires are raging over almost 4,000 hectares, destroying fynbos, wildlife and people's homes. Thick clouds of smoke are hanging over the Atlantic Seaboard and Table Mountain, while fire fighters have been busy trying to tame the fires for the last four days. Maddy just contacted me in despair (she lives in Fish Hoek) to inform me that the distress signals from the animals, wildlife, pets and horses alike, are so overwhelming that she had become physically ill. At this very moment she is trying to help and calm the horses on a big horse farm in Noordhoek. At the same time, Mario, who lives on the other side of the mountain and cannot reach the disaster area because the roads are closed, is sending protection and healing energy to the area and is communicating with the angels to help. I think that even if people do not understand or believe in Mario and Maddy's gifts, the knowledge that their intentions are good and that they are trying to help, should be enough.

Mario

'It is said that knowledge that is implemented, is wisdom. I am currently busy practising and using all I have learned during my spiritual journey so far. I am teaching others how to do the same. I have my own crystal business, called 'Angel Rocks' and am selling all kinds of polished and natural raw crystals, handmade crystal jewellery and my own home made natural bath salts. I still work in the film industry to 'pay the bills', but have shifted my focus on working more as a holistic practitioner. I am closely involved with a holistic shop in Durbanville and work from there doing healing, counselling and teaching. I present workshops and retreats and act as guest speaker on various occasions as well as on radio and TV from time to time. I have started to develop and work on more spiritual abilities than just my sense of feeling and still learn more about it every day.'

Maddy

'Through the past few years, working with horses and the other animals on the farm, my gift to communicate with animals has advanced a lot. I have decided to use all my gifts for the benefit of the animal kingdom, because animals are my true passion in life. I want to help people to understand the animals they are living with or are in touch with, to better the relationships between humans and animals. I believe that humans can learn a lot about and from animals, which could make the world a better place for both species to co-exist in harmony.'

'I have started to work as a professional animal behaviourist and animal 'whisperer' and started my own business named 'Maddy's Ark', which I believe says it all. I want it to be a safe haven for animals and animal lovers alike, to understand each other better. I ache to help owners to really understand their pets and to learn how to improve their relationships with them. I do house sitting for pets, do healing with animals that are ill, do animal tapping and many more, whichever comes my way. As a qualified game ranger, I am also a very good wildlife tracker and spotter, because of my ability to see and feel the energy, before anything else.'

'My dream has come true and I am now at the beginning of a life long journey….. to walk and talk with animals. And this I can promise, I WILL walk my talk.'

ABOUT THE AUTHOR

Dalene studied Education and Teaching and has been a teacher for children with special needs, for fifteen years. She then completed her Master's Degree in Play Therapy. After her divorce she started lecturing Early Child Development and Educational Psychology at a collage in Stellenbosch, near Cape Town. Her husband died in 2006 and she became the single parent of Mario and Maddy, the co-authors of this book.

Mario is a qualified photographer and is working as a movie and commercial cast coordinator. He is also a life coach and spiritual councilor as well as a healer. He presents workshops and various topics like spiritual awareness, angels and healing.

Maddy is a qualified game ranger and field guide. She is an animal healer and can also communicate with animals. She teaches people about animal behavior and rehabilitates them to live in harmony.